ROADMAP TO A NEW NORMAL SAFE SCHOOL

STRATEGIES TO FOLLOW

DR DHEERAJ MEHROTRA

XpressPublishing
An imprint of Notion Press

XpressPublishing
An imprint of Notion Press

No.8, 3rd Cross Street,CIT Colony,
Mylapore, Chennai, Tamil Nadu-600004

ISBN 978-1-63669-330-9

The work is dedicated to all Educators,
Students & Parents who effortlessly took
the challenges during the lockdown and
explored the situation as an opportunity
to learn.

Towards A Safer World

Contents

Foreword   *vii*

Preface   *ix*

Acknowledgements   *xi*

1. Guidelines And Strategies For Schools   1

2. About The Author   25

3. Books By The Same Author   28

Foreword

The book encapsulates the need for the novel practices by schools globally to face the new normal.

The priority is towards SAFETY and SECURITY of our kids!

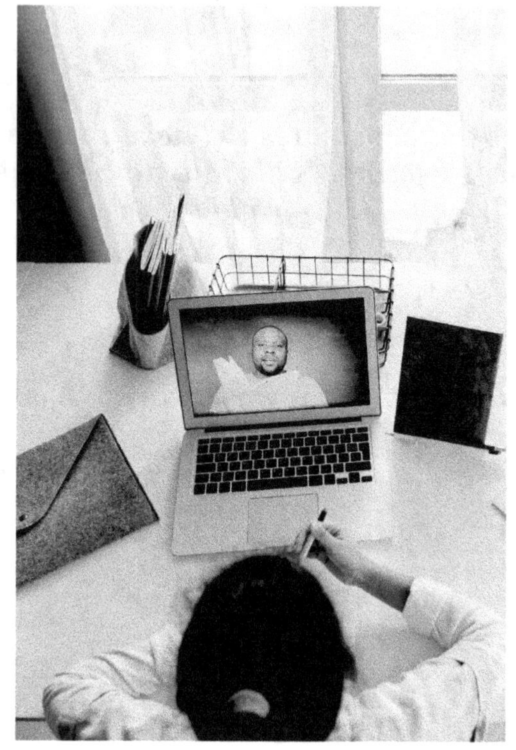

Making Learning A Priority

Preface

Roadmap To A New Normal Safe School defines the priority by the educators to explore safety guidelines and make learning innovative without fear for our kids in particular.

It serves as a guide and a ready reckoner to explore the effective management of the teaching and learning process.

I am sure the effectiveness shall be followed religiously.

Best & Cheers!

Dr Dheeraj Mehrotra

www.authordheerajmehrotra.com

Acknowledgements

I share my heartful thanks to all the wonderful teachers who have been kind enough to undertake the responsibility of going online and accepting the challenges towards teaching with no experience of the new environment. I salute those edu warriors for making learning so easy and comfortable for the students through technology in just no time.

The webinars, online assignments, projects and interface worked so well with the preparedness and the ability to perform for their kids, make our teachers really special.

I thank them and dedicate this work to them.

CHAPTER ONE

Guidelines And Strategies For Schools

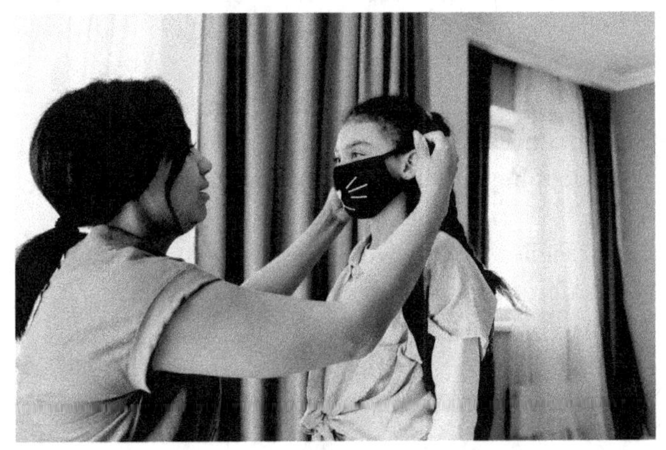

#1

Assure Sick Students, Teachers and other staff should not come to school at any cost.

#2

Enforce regular hand washing with safe water and soap, alcohol rub/ hand sanitizer or chlorine solution.

#3

Assure daily disinfection and cleaning of the school surfaces.

#4

The schools must Provide water, sanitation and waste management facilities and should follow environmental cleaning and decontamination procedures.

#5

A teachers' regular meeting every week to assure safety rules and regulations to be followed.

#6
The staff has to understand the basic information about COVID-19, including its symptoms as know the latest facts and its complications including how it is transmitted and how to prevent transmission.

#7

The Schools need to follow environmental cleaning and decontamination procedures as a habit.

#8

Stay rooted to the UNICEF and WHO and other national ministry advisories via awareness e-newsletters.

#9

The Staff should be aware of fake information or the myths that may circulate by word-of-mouth or online via whatsapp messages.

#10

The schools must update the school emergency plans and share the information via messages, videos and pictures.

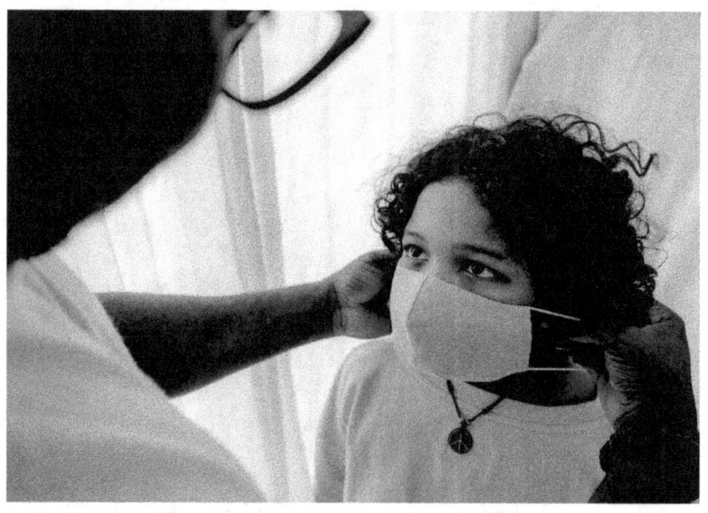

#11

The schools should avoid any community events/ meetings scheduled on school premises on priority.

#12

The schools must reinforce frequent handwashing and sanitation and procure the needed supplies as a priority.

#13

There should be clean and disinfect school buildings in place with classrooms being sanitized once a day particularly the places touched regularly by the kids like railings, handles etc.

#14

Social Distancing should be standardised with NO to school assemblies, sports games and Yoga.

#15

Practical should be conducted with social distancing norms.

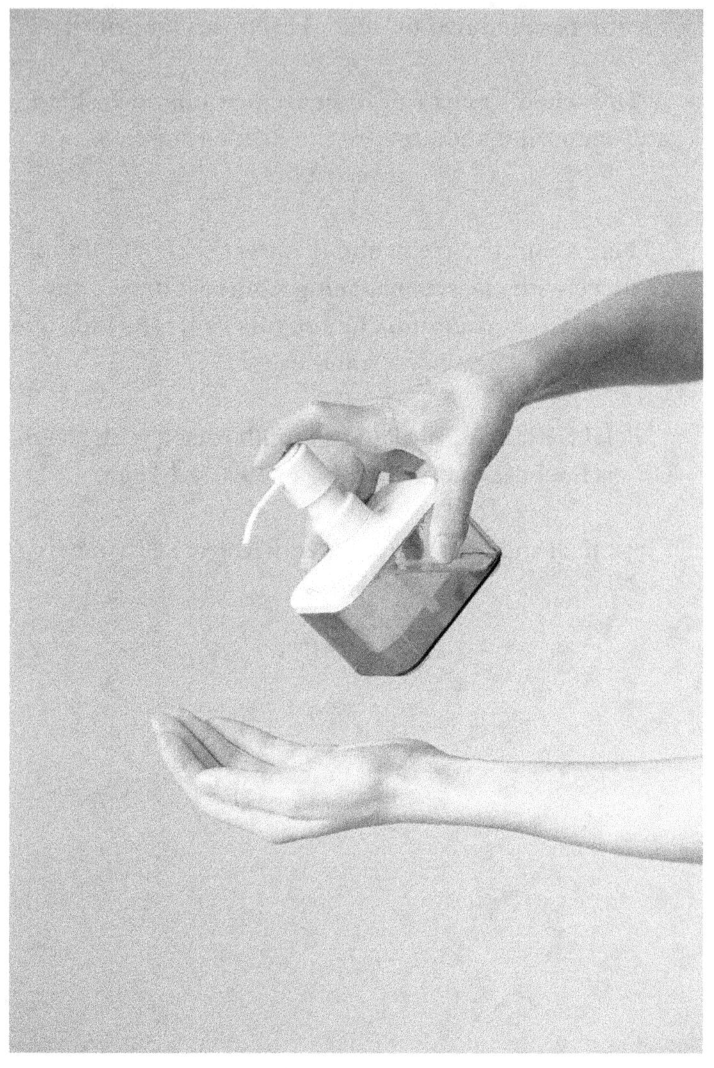

#16

Washrooms should be marked NOT FOR USE and provide use alternatively with a gap marked NOT FOR USE on priority.

#17

In the classrooms, create space for children's desks to be at least one metre apart. The space must be created avoiding unnecessary touching.

#18

There has to be an established procedure if the staff or the students become unwell. We need to plan ahead with the school health staff to cater to the need analysis.

#19

Information Sharing needs to be a priority as per the health and education authorities. We need to share the information related to the disease, prevention and control efforts being taken on revision by the school.

#20

The schools must ensure online communication channel to be stronger and updated with proper backup of data cloud and software update.

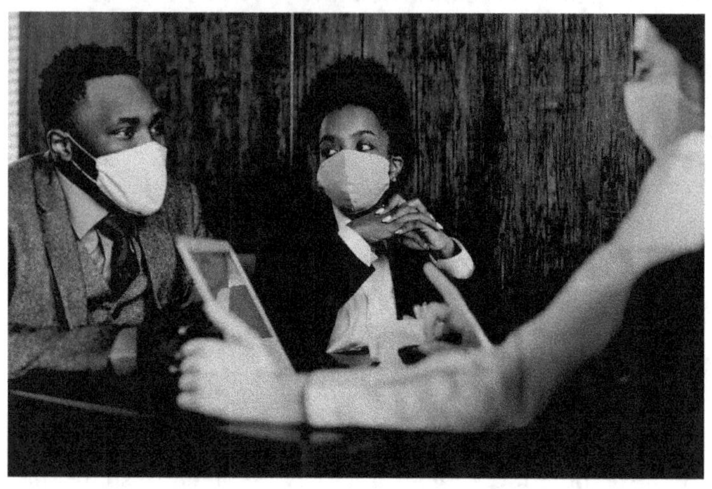

#21
Monitor the school attendance and track the participation of the staff and the students and take measures to ensure the regular health updates.

#22
Regular online teaching should be followed for the students who by any reason are not able to attend the school physically.

#23
Teachers should engage with updated and street smart teaching strategies using various creative and innovative teaching platforms online.

#24
To engage students, the teachers must assign reading and exercises for home study on a regular basis.

#25

Schools must promote podcasts, radio/ TV/ as an optional to Internet based in addition.

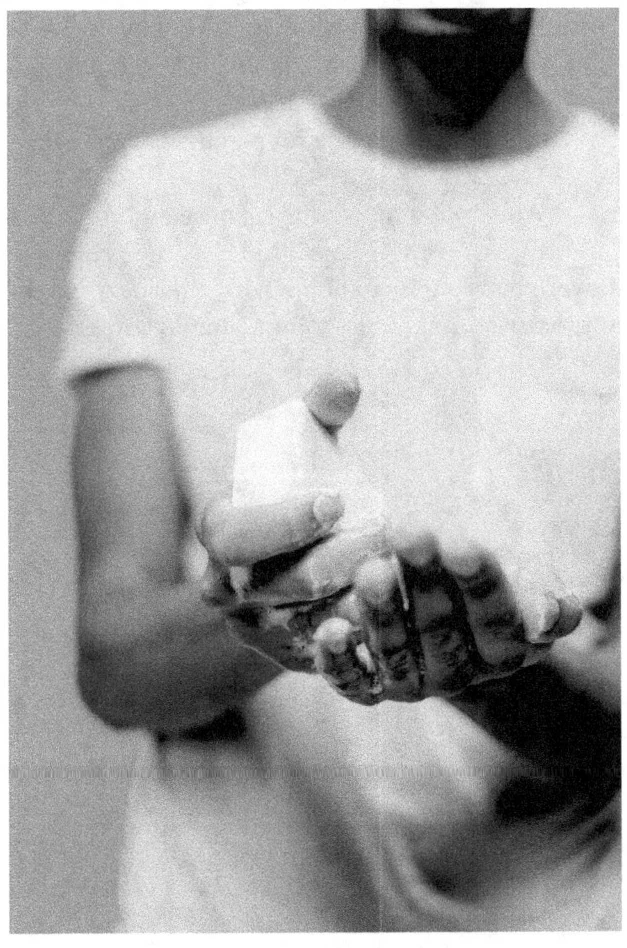

#26
Schools can promote their RADIO FM transmission for imparting lessons. This can be an independent

exercise or can be streamed with existing channels.

#27

Schools may assign the co-ordinators/ head teachers to ensure follow up of learning both via physical as well as remote based learning outcomes regularly.

#28

Avoid close contact with people who are sick.

#29

Avoid touching your eyes, nose and mouth.

#30

Cover your cough or sneeze with a tissue, then throw the tissue in the thrash immediately after use.

#31

The schools need to assure the restroom signage posted detailing COVID-19 recommendations and students must be asked to practice these recommendations fervently.

#32

The teachers must implement targeted health education through the integration of disease prevention and control in daily activities and lessons.

#33

Engage Students in positive thoughts, interactions, questions and concerns.

#34

Assure clean and disinfection of school buildings using sodium hypochlorite at 0.5% for disinfecting surfaces and 70% ethyl alcohol for disinfection of small items.

#35

Teachers should be made comfortable towards regular use of online/ distance learning to be the preferred mode of teaching and should be encouraged.

#36

The students should not be forced to send their wards. Always prefer the consent from them to assure regular participation. Attendance must not be enforced.

#37

Schools need to follow the SOP issued by the Education Department of the States/ authorities.

#38

Ensure the availability of thermometers, disinfectants, soaps with proper upkeep and calibration.

#39

Schools should form Task Teams like Emergency Care/ Support/ Response Team, General Support Team/

Commodity Support Team with Teachers and Parents as representatives.

#40

Mark the roll number wise seating plan for the students with 6 feet distance between students.

#41

Schools need to ensure social distancing at the Entry and Exit Points of the School on priority. Earmark different lanes for exit and entry. Use Public Address System to convey the information.

#42

Assure display of signages and marking for enforcing physical/ social distancing and safety protocols. This may be done in classrooms, washrooms, libraries, lobbies.

#43

Strictly ban on spitting in public for the students.

#44

Schools must avoid events for some time where the physical or the social distancing is difficult or simply not possible as a precautionary measure.

#45

Schools must adopt online admissions/ payment of fees/ issue of homework assignments.

#46

Schools should promote VIRTUAL PARENT TEACHER meetings on a regular basis.

#47

Regular Virtual Meetings should be given a priority with the parents class wise with the subject teachers and the Head of the school to ease concerns.

#48

Schools should consider work from home for all employees who are at higher risk.

#49

Medical Room must have a full time health care attendant/ nurse/ doctor and a counsellor at all time during school hours to attend to the students in the time of need.

#50

Schools should promote the prescribed cut in syllabus if any and reduce the course for the home based exams to build confidence of the students.

#51

Schools must invest on stronger and good quality Wi-Fi Connections/ Digital Platforms.

#52

Schools must ensure and educate children not to exchange masks with others and wear them at all times.

#53

Students need to be told that they should avoid sharing of their tiffin for the time being. They should eat only of their own tiffin.

#54

Schools must ensure no vendors/ canteen to be operative for some time. To avoid infection.

#55

Regular sanitization of school transportation must be ensured at least twice a day and the staff should ensure physical distancing among students.

#56

Schools should form teams to supervise the crowd during the morning and afternoon shifts. Students should be placed at marked/ allocated places for the pick-up/ drop.

#57

Schools must ensure not to share any books/ notes/ tiffin/ water bottle/ stationary with any other student for the time being.

#58

Schools must also ensure to provide different FOOD Breaks for different classes.

#59

Overcrowding in the washrooms should also be discouraged as a priority.

#60

Schools must not collect the waste instead an adequate waste disposal system has to be initiated on priority.

#61

Schools must plan non-stressing assessments to identify the learning gaps. This shall also give them confidence to learn better and engaged.

#62

Happiness Class/ Mindfulness/ Meditation should be a part of the class based assembly on priority.

#63

Regular class visits by the Head of the school should be made to sensitize all the students about the pandemic and its related myths, social stigma, fears and precautions in particular.

#64

Students should be encouraged to avoid JUNK food as a practice and take healthy food, fruits and do regular yoga to boost their immunity.

#65

Regular Trainings must be conducted both online and classroom based for the staff to you the digital platforms as an add on mechanism for the teaching in practice.

#66

Provisions should be in place to cater to the needs of the Special Children as well. A dedicated teacher should be there to assure their comfort and safety.

#67

Schools should promote project-based learning assignments, portfolios, creative work.

#68

Schools must implement and re-adjust the school calendar with classroom based inputs and climate. The transition shall take some time.

#69

Schools must promote VOCATIONAL education with subject related options.

#70

Schools should work for the MENTAL HEALTH and EMOTIONAL SAFETY of the children and MUSIC plays a wider role here. Music teachers need to ensure soothing music during the starting of the school and in the last period.

#71

Schools may reduce the class sizes with alternate day classes.

#72

Schools may also stagger the opening and closing hours of school to avoid an influx of parents and students at the school gates and at the parking.

#73

Regular periods for teaching and promoting Hygiene Practices need to be followed by schools. They need to be taught the correct way to wash their hands and dispose of tissues properly.

#74

Schools must ensure to encourage students to use their personal transport as far as possible for some time.

#75

Schools must encourage their teachers to practice and review of subjects covered by online means to gather confidence among the learners.

#76

Schools must also ensure regular medical screening of school drivers, support staff.

#77

All couriers and other goods received at the main gate of the school should be set aside for the prescribed disinfecting period regularly.

#78

The schools must provide PPE Kits for the health care workers to tackle any unforeseen situations.

#79

Schools should be YES to all safeguarding readiness towards investment. A regular connect with the parents to provide all preparedness is must to assure their confidence.

#80

Schools must promote use of VIRTUAL labs.

#81

Schools may opt for sanitizing tunnel to walk through where students may walk with a minimum 4 feet distance from the nearest peer and sit at a distance from the next child.

#82

Schools must have staggered lunch-time to reduce crowding at eating places.

#83

Students particularly the senior students may be permitted to download school applications on their mobile phones and can be allowed to bring their laptops at times to assist tech-driven learning if possible.

#84

Schools must use social distancing floor stickers at all important places.

#85

Schools must take precautions to shield vulnerable staff and pupils.

#86

Avoid creating two-way traffic in school hallways and corridors.

#87

Schools must talk regularly to the students about the importance of wearing a face mask and model wearing them as a family.

#88

Students should be counselled to clean their hands before and after touching their mask.

#89

Schools must limit the mixing of classes for school and after-school activities.

#90

Schools may stagger the school day to vary the start and end times and avoid having all the students and teachers together at once.

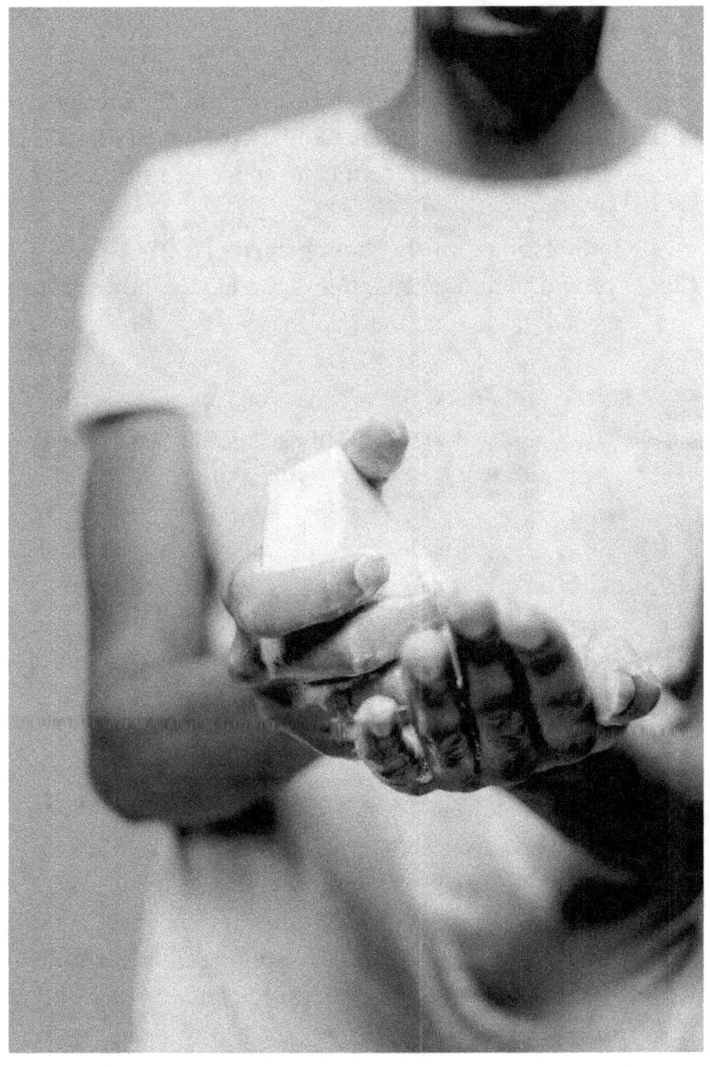

#91

Schools must encourage students not to gather and socialize in larger groups upon leaving the school grounds.

#92

Teachers should ensure, if by accident the students cough or sneeze on their hands, instruct them to immediately wash their hands or apply hand sanitizer.

#93

Schools need to check on priority NOT TO MIX Cleaners and disinfectants unless the labels indicate it is safe to do so.

#94

The schools need to curate some fun and creative ideas and rules for avoiding high-risk and high-touch areas in the classroom/ school.

#95

Schools may consider holding classes and activities outside as much as possible as low risk reassure.

#96

Schools must use communication methods that are accessible for all students, faculty and staff including those with disabilities.

#97

Schools must broadcast regular announcements on reducing the spread of COVID-19 on Public Address Systems.

#98

Teachers should assure discouraging of items to be used by students that are difficult to clean or disinfect.

#99

Schools should consider ventilation system upgrades to increase the delivery of clean air and dilute the potential contaminants in the classrooms.

**BUY
UDEMY COURSE
On
Tackling the Post Pandemic Within Schools**
*Getting Prepared To Face
the Challenges ahead*

This course includes:

30-Day Money-Back Guarantee

- 41 mins on-demand video
- Full lifetime access
- Access on mobile and TV
- Certificate of completion

https://www.udemy.com/share/102YCc/

CHAPTER TWO

About the Author

Dheeraj Mehrotra, MS, MPhil, Ph.D. (Education Management) honoris causa., a white and a yellow belt in SIX SIGMA, a Certified NLP Business Diploma holder, is an Educational Innovator, Author, with expertise in Six Sigma In Education, Academic Audits, Neuro Linguistic Programming (NLP), Total Quality Management In Education, an Experiential Educator, a CBSE Resource towards School Assessment (SQAA), CCE, JIT, Five S and KAIZEN. He has authored over 40 books on Computer Science for ICSE/ ISC/ CBSE Students, over 10 books of academic interest for the field of education excellence and Six Sigma. A former Principal at De Indian Public School, New Delhi, (INDIA) with an ample teaching experience of over Two Decades, he is a certified Trainer for Quality Circles/ TQM in Education and QCI Standards for School Accreditation/ Six Sigma in Education. He has also been honored with the President of India's National Teacher Award in the year 2006 and the Best Science Teacher State Award (By the Ministry of Science and Technology, State of UP), Innovation in Education for his inception of Six Sigma In Education by Education Watch, New Delhi and Education World- Best Teacher Award, BOLT Learner Teacher Award by Air India, 'Innovation in Education Award 2016' by Higher Education Forum (HEF), Gujarat Chapter, among others. He has developed over 150 FREE EDUCATIONAL MOBILE Apps for the Google Play Store exclusively for Teachers, Students and Parents. This work has been recognized by the LIMCA BOOK OF RECORDS & INDIA BOOK OF RECORDS as the only Indian to draw that feast. Dr. Mehrotra is presently working as an Academic Evangelist in India. He has conducted over 1000 workshops globally on "Excellence In Education" integrated with Total Quality Management and Six Sigma, Technology Integration in Education (TIE), Developing towards being ROCKSTAR TEACHERS, including Cyberspace, Cyber Security, Classroom Management, School Leadership & Management and Innovative teaching within classrooms via Mind Maps, NLP and Experiential Learning in Academics. He is an active TEDx speaker and can be viewed at youtube tedX channel. A UDEMY Premium

Instructor, Dr. Mehrotra has published over 300 online courses on UDEMY.COM making him one of the widely known instructors from India with over 7,00,000 students globally.

He can be visited at www.authordheerajmehrotra.com

CHAPTER THREE

Books by the Same Author

Available at
www.authordheerajmehrotra.com & www.amazon.in

AI
ARTIFICIAL
INTELLIGENCE
BASICS FOR
SCHOOL
STUDENTS
(Class IX)
As per the LATEST
CBSE CURRICULUM (Code No. 417)
DR. DHEERAJ MEHROTRA

NLP
FOR TEACHERS
Towards Quality Teaching Skills
Dr. Dheeraj Mehrotra

100 GREEN SCHOOLING IDEAS
TOWARDS A SUSTAINABLE CULTURE IN SCHOOLS
Dr. Dheeraj Mehrotra

BASICS OF
ARTIFICIAL
INTELLIGENCE
&
MACHINE
LEARNING
Dr. DHEERAJ MEHROTRA

DR. JAGDISH
GANDHI
The Quality
Education Icon!
DR. DHEERAJ MEHROTRA

TOWARDS EXCELLENCE IN
TEACHING & LEARNING
200
WOW TEACHING
IDEAS
DR. DHEERAJ MEHROTRA

SECURING SAFETY & QUALITY CARING
99 SAFETY AND
SECURITY
ANCHORS WITHIN SCHOOLS
DR. DHEERAJ MEHROTRA

Available at www.authordheerajmehrotra.comFor
Comments & Feedbacktqmhead@aol.com